STARTING TECHNOLOGY

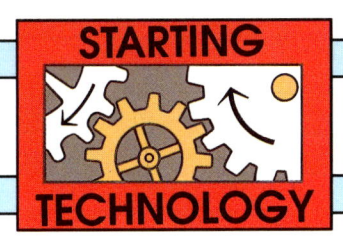

COLOUR AND LIGHT

John Williams

Illustrated by
Malcolm S. Walker

Wayland

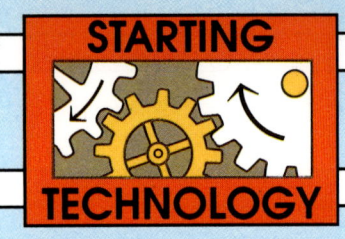

Titles in this series

AIR
COLOUR AND LIGHT
ELECTRICITY
FLIGHT
MACHINES
TIME
WATER
WHEELS

Words printed in **bold** appear in the glossary on page 30

© Copyright 1991 Wayland (Publishers) Ltd

First published in 1991 by
Wayland (Publishers) Ltd
61 Western Road, Hove
East Sussex BN3 1JD, England

Editor: Anna Girling
Designer: Kudos Design Services

British Library Cataloguing in Publication Data
Williams, John
   Colour and light.
   1. Colour
   I. Title II. Walker, Malcolm *1947-* III. Series
   535.6

   ISBN 0 7502 0170 3

Typeset by Kudos Editorial and Design Services, Sussex, England
Printed in Italy by Rotolito Lombarda S.p.A.
Bound in Belgium by Casterman S.A.

CONTENTS

Looking at Light	4
Mixing Colours	6
Colour Projects	8
Spinning Circles	10
Where Is It?	12
Tie-Dye	14
Mirrors	16
Periscopes	18
Shadows	20
Slides	22
Bigger and Better	24
Playing with Light	26
Notes for Parents and Teachers	28
Glossary	30
Books to Read	31
Index	32

STARTING TECHNOLOGY

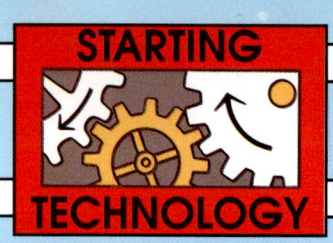

LOOKING AT LIGHT

Can you imagine living in a black and white world? There would be no green grass, no blue sky and no bright clothes. Everything would be black, white or grey. It would be very dull.

Most of our natural light comes from sunshine. This is made up of seven colours — the colours of the **rainbow**. They are: red, orange, yellow, green, blue, **indigo** and violet. There are three main colours: red, green and blue. The others are mixtures of these.

Try to pick out the seven colours in this rainbow.

Experimenting with light

You will need:

A **prism**
A bowl of water
Thin cooking oil
Paper and pencils

Sunlight

1. Look through the prism.
Hold it close to your eyes.
Can you see colours shining through?

2. Pour a little oil on the top of the water. Look for the same colours you saw through the prism.

Sunlight

3. Collect as many different materials as you can. Try paper, tissue paper, wood, metal and plastic. Hold them up to the light. Can you see through them? Can you see shadows through them? Make a chart like this.

NAME OF MATERIAL	CAN SEE THROUGH	CAN SEE SHADOWS THROUGH	CANNOT SEE THROUGH
Tissue paper		✓	
Wood			✓
Glass	✓		

Things that you can see through, like glass windows, are called **transparent**.

Further work

Red, green and blue are called the **primary colours** of sunlight. Take a sheet of see-through plastic (such as acetate) in each of these colours. Hold them up to the light. Put one on top of another. What colours do you see?

Collect as many coloured see-through sweet and food wrappers as you can. Make a pattern or picture with them by sticking them on to a sheet of tracing paper. Fix your picture to a window.

5

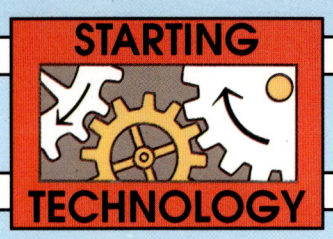

STARTING TECHNOLOGY: MIXING COLOURS

As we have seen, the primary colours of sunlight are red, green and blue. Red and green together make yellow. Red, green and blue together make white.

The primary colours of painting are different. They are red, yellow and blue. Mixed together, these make dark brown.

These children have used different mixtures of colours for their paintings.

Paints and dyes

You will need:

Paper
Paintbrushes
Red, yellow and blue paints
Food **dyes** (red, yellow, blue and green)
Transparent bowl of water

1. Draw pictures with any two primary colours. What other colours do these make when mixed together?

2. Now paint a picture using all three primary colours.

3. Put one or two drops of one of your food dyes into the bowl of water. Wait to see what happens when the dye mixes with the water. **Do not shake the bowl.** Now try with other colours.

STARTING TECHNOLOGY

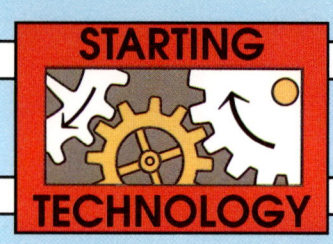

COLOUR PROJECTS

Making a colour box

You will need:

A shoe box
Card
Felt-tip pens
Scissors
Glue
Coloured sheets of acetate

1. Draw and colour a picture on one end of the box, on the inside.

2. Draw more pictures on card, cut them out and stick them just in front of the main picture, standing upright.

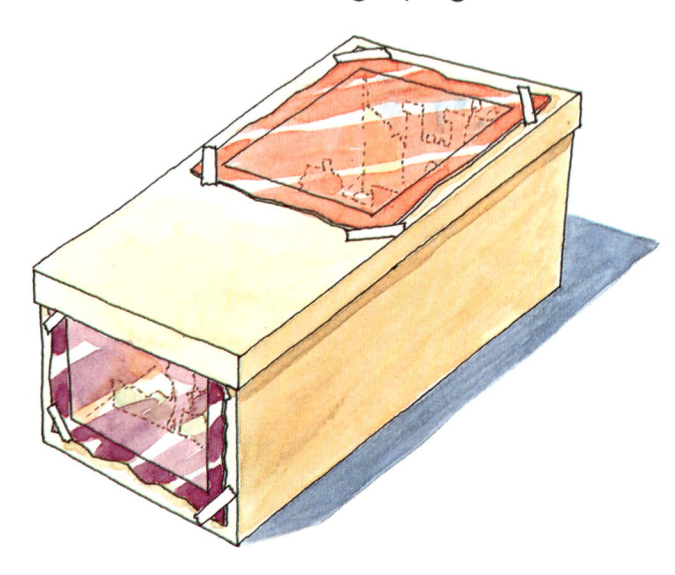

3. Cut a square hole in the lid of the box. Cut another hole at the front end of the box.

4. Stick coloured acetate over the holes. What colour does your picture look now?

Making a pair of spectacles

You will need:

Card
Scissors
Glue
Coloured sheets of acetate

1. Cut out a frame for your spectacles from card, making sure it fits your face.

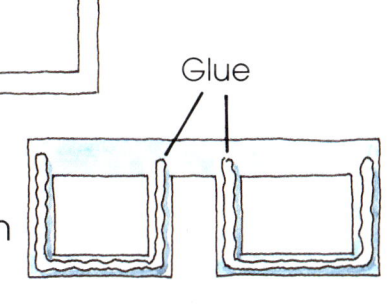

2. Cut out another piece of card, exactly the same as the main front part of the frame.

3. Glue this to the spectacles, but leave the top side open.

4. Cut out pieces of acetate and slide them into the top of the spectacles. Try different colours.

Look at the colours in this glass window. Light shines through the glass to show up the coloured pattern.

STARTING TECHNOLOGY

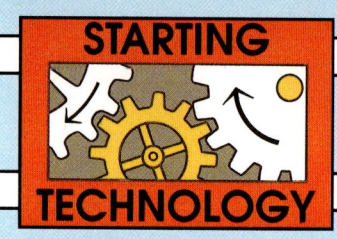

SPINNING CIRCLES

Making coloured spinners

You will need:

Card
Felt-tip pens or crayons
A ruler
Pieces of **dowel**, 10 cm long
Scissors

1. Draw a circle on card, about 12 cm in **diameter**, and cut it out.

2. Draw lines through the middle of the circle, so that it has eight parts all about the same size. Colour four parts blue and four parts yellow.

3. Push a piece of dowel through the middle of the circle, so that you can spin it. You will need to sharpen one end of the dowel. **Ask an adult to help you do this.**

4. Set the circle spinning on the floor or a table top. Can you still see the different colours? What colour did you think you could see?

Further work

Cut out some more circles and draw different patterns on them, using different colours. Do they all look the same when they are spinning?

This coloured top is like your spinning circles. Its colours blur as it goes round.

11

STARTING TECHNOLOGY

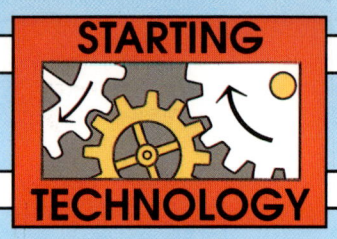

WHERE IS IT?

Many animals use colour to make themselves difficult to see. This is called **camouflage**. Some animals try to be the same colour as the things around them. Others may be spotted or striped. Spots and stripes make an animal's shape difficult to see from a distance.

Can you see the little tree frog? It is the same colour as the leaf it is sitting on.

Making camouflaged animals

You will need:

Card
Felt-tip pens or paints
Glue
Scissors
Drawing pins

1. Draw some coloured pictures of different types of scenery. You might draw a forest, lots of tall grass, pebbles and rocks, or an underwater picture. Do not draw any animals in your pictures.

2. Draw some animals that you think would live in the type of scenery you have painted. Colour them carefully to match your scenery pictures. Cut them out and stick a small strip of card to them so that you can hold them up.

3. Pin your scenery pictures to the wall and hold the animals up in front. Ask a friend to stand away from the pictures and tell you which animals are hard to see. Remember, camouflage does not make an animal invisible, just more difficult to see.

STARTING TECHNOLOGY

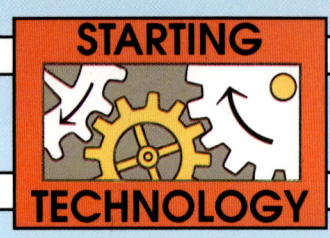

TIE-DYE

Tying and dyeing

You will need:

Some white cotton cloth
String
Rubber bands
Marbles
Cold-water dyes
Scissors

WARNING: Never use an iron on your own. Always ask an adult to help you.

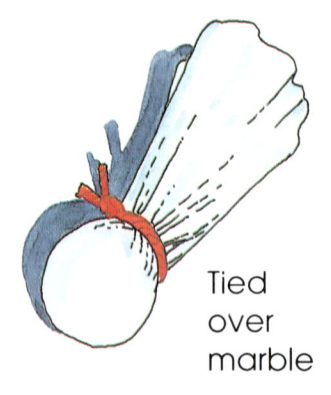

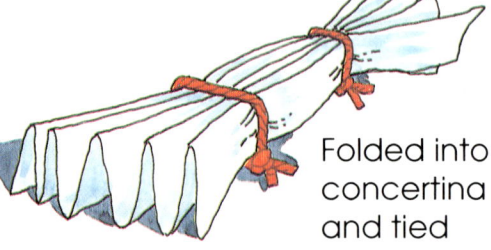

1. Cut out some pieces of cloth, about the size of a large handkerchief.

2. Fold them, each in a different way, and tie string or rubber bands round them tightly. You could tie them into a parcel, fold them into a concertina, knot them, twist them, or tie them over a marble.

Tied over marble

Tied into parcel

Folded into concertina and tied

Knotted

Twisted and tied

14

3. Soak the cloths in water and then put them into the dye solution (following the instructions on the dye packet). When using dyes, it is a good idea to wear an overall and plastic gloves to protect your clothes and skin.

4. Rinse the cloths in water again, untie them and leave them on a flat plastic surface to dry.

5. When they are dry, they will need to be ironed to make the dye stay in the cloth.

Further work

Different folds and ties make different patterns. On a larger piece of cloth draw a pattern that you would like to make. Use the patterns you have already made as guides. Tie your cloth to make the pattern and then dye it as before.

STARTING TECHNOLOGY

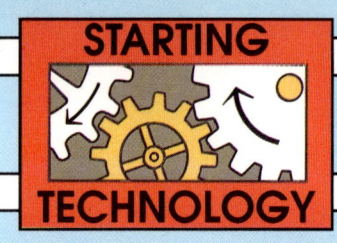

MIRRORS

Make a collection of shiny things. You could look for metal spoons, glass objects, beads or tin foil. Can you see yourself in any of them?

Look at yourself in a large shiny spoon. Turn the spoon around. Do you look the same from both sides? A shiny spoon acts as a curved mirror.

This is a pattern made by a kaleidoscope.

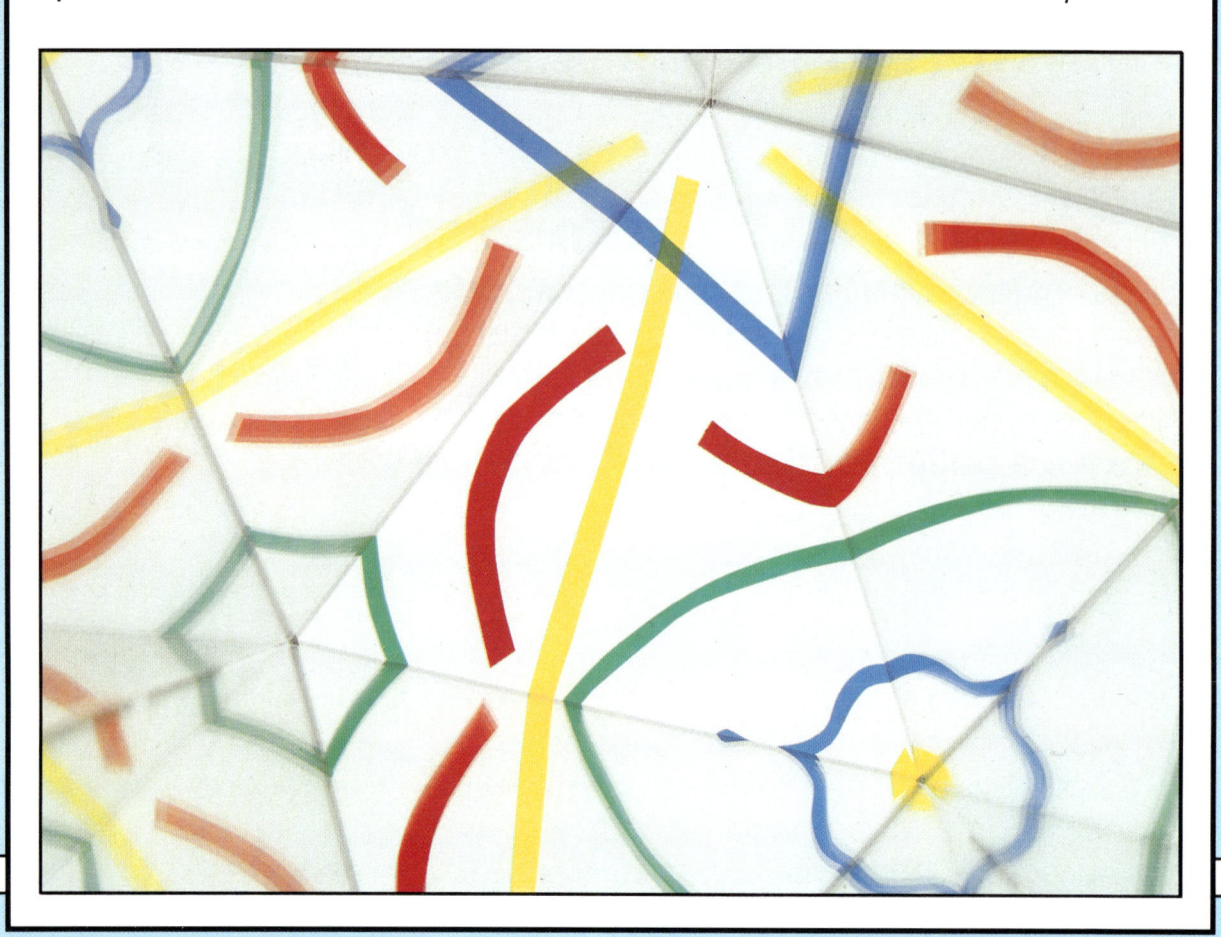

Making a kaleidoscope

You will need:

Three small plastic mirrors, all the same size
Card
Sticky tape
Tracing paper
Scissors
Sequins or small beads

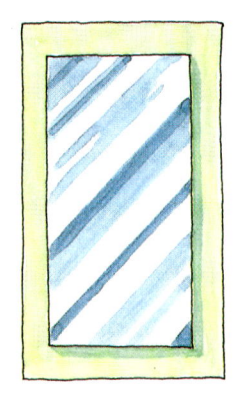

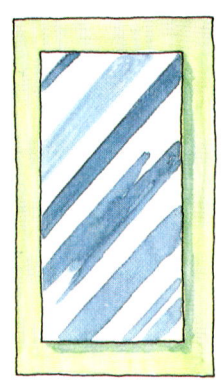

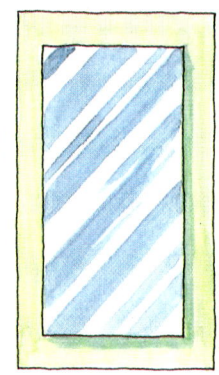

1. Cut out three pieces of card, a little larger than the mirrors. Stick them to the backs of the mirrors.

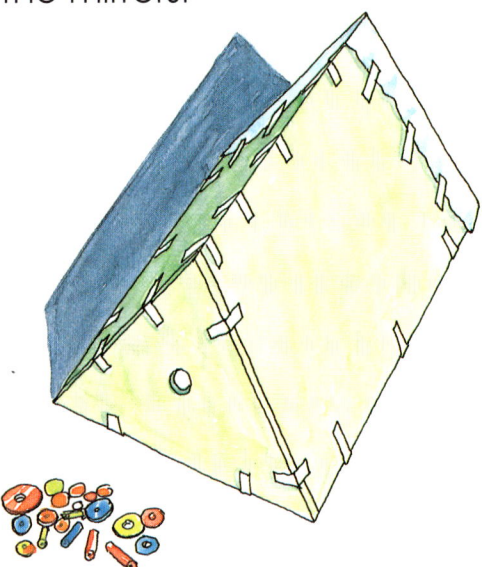

2. Stick the pieces of card together at the edges, so that they make a triangular-shaped tube with the mirrors on the inside.

3. At one end stick a triangle of card, with a small peep-hole in the middle. At the other end, stick a piece of tracing paper. Put the sequins into the kaleidoscope, through the hole.

4. Look through the peep-hole to see what patterns the three mirrors make.

5. You can decorate the outside of your kaleidoscope by painting coloured patterns on it.

17

STARTING TECHNOLOGY

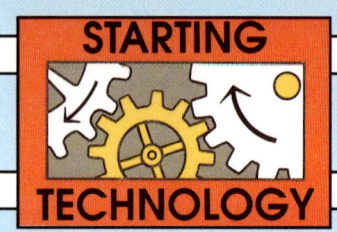

PERISCOPES

Hold two mirrors in front of you, one above the other. Tilt them so that when you look in the bottom mirror you can see what is **reflected** by the top mirror. A periscope in a **submarine** uses mirrors like this to see what is above the water.

It is often helpful to be able to see round corners. This mirror is positioned to help drivers see if a car is coming round a bend.

18

Making a periscope

You will need:

Two mirrors, both the same size
Thick card
Glue
Scissors

1. Cut out two pieces of card, 70 cm long and the same width as your mirrors. Make a fold 10 cm from the end of each piece of card.

2. Glue the mirrors to the pieces of card, across the folds. They should both be fixed at exactly the same slant.

3. At the other end of each piece of card cut a square hole.

4. Glue the two pieces together so that the mirrors are at either end.

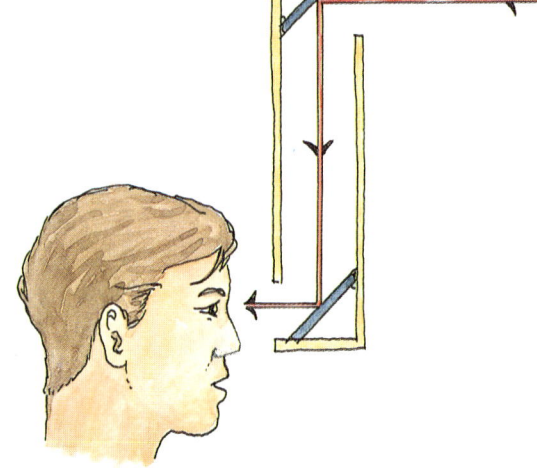

5. Cut two more pieces of card for the sides and glue them to your periscope.

6. Hold the periscope upright and look through the bottom hole. What do you see?

10 cm

19

STARTING TECHNOLOGY

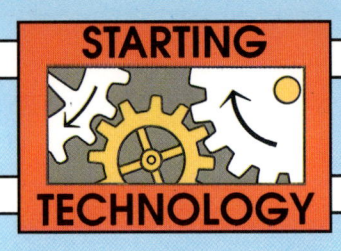

SHADOWS

Go outside on a sunny day. Look at your shadow. Is it a funny shape? Is it taller than you or shorter than you? Can you jump on your own shadow?

These shadows are very long. What time of day do you think it is?

Making a shadow theatre

You will need:

A large shoe box
Card
Tracing paper
Sticky tape
Scissors
A torch

1. Cut a large square hole in one end of the box. Stick a piece of tracing paper over this end.

2. Cut a smaller round hole at the other end. Cut narrow slits across the bottom of the box.

3. Draw some people and objects on card and cut them out. Slide them through the slits into the box.

4. Shine a torch through the round hole at the end of the box. Look for shadows on the tracing paper screen at the other end. Do the shadows change when you move the torch further away from the box?

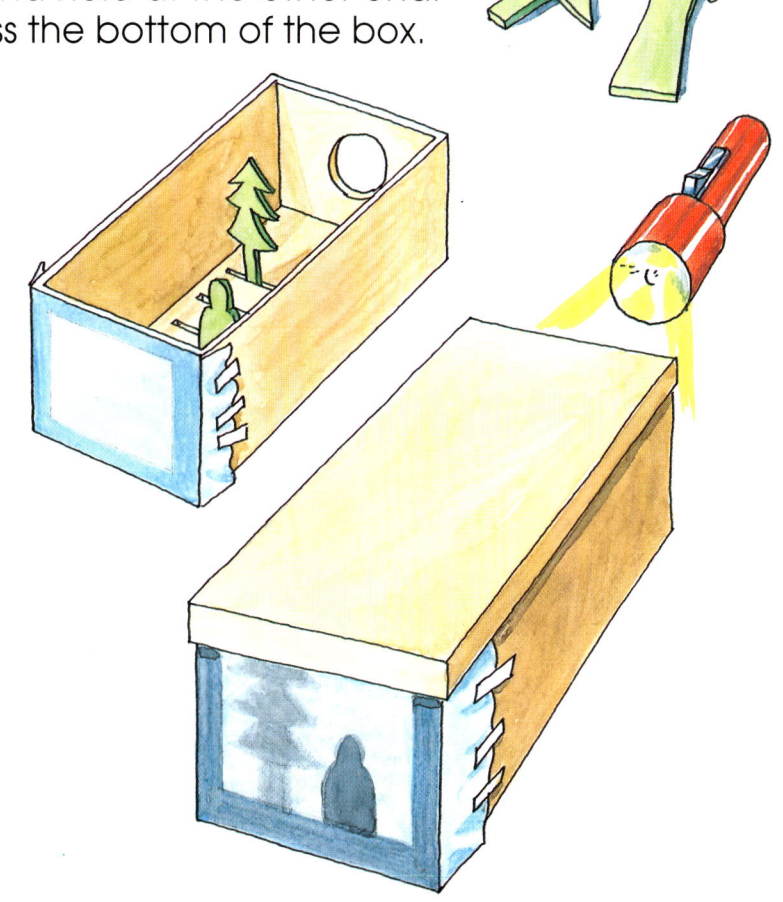

STARTING TECHNOLOGY

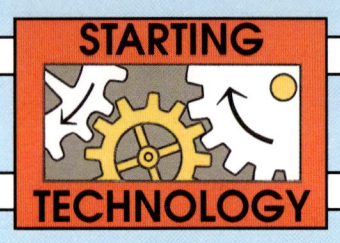

SLIDES

Have you seen a slide show at school or at a museum? A machine called a **projector** is used to show pictures on a wall or screen.

Look how much bigger the people in this picture are when they are seen through a magnifying glass.

Making a simple projector

You will need:

Card
Felt-tip pens
A sheet of see-through plastic, such as acetate
Glue or sticky tape
A magnifying glass
A torch

1. Cut out a square frame from the card.

2. Cut out a square of plastic and draw a picture on it. Stick it to the frame.

3. Hold the picture and the magnifying glass up in front of a white wall.

4. Ask a friend to shine a torch so that the light goes through the picture, then the magnifying glass and on to the wall.

5. Move the picture and glass nearer and then further away from the wall. Does the picture change?

STARTING TECHNOLOGY

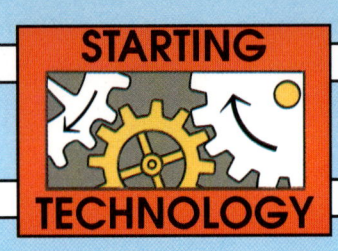

BIGGER AND BETTER

A microscope uses **lenses** to make small things look bigger. A telescope uses lenses to make things that are far away look nearer.

Making a simple microscope

You will need:

A strip of thick card, about 20 cm long and 5 cm wide
A newspaper
A sewing needle
Some water

1. Make folds in the card, 4 cm from each end, so that it forms a kind of bridge.

2. Make a hole in the middle of the card with the needle.

3. Put your 'microscope' on to a page of the newspaper. Put your eye close to the hole and look for a letter on the page.

4. Put a small drop of water on the card, over the hole. Look again through the hole. Gently move the folded ends in and out. Does this change the way the letter looks?

Making telescopes

You will need:

Magnifying lenses
A flat strip of wood,
  about 30 cm long
Plasticine
Two cardboard tubes, one
  slightly larger than the other

1. Lenses come in different shapes. The ones you need are called **convex** lenses. Both sides are curved outwards. You will need a thick and a thin one.

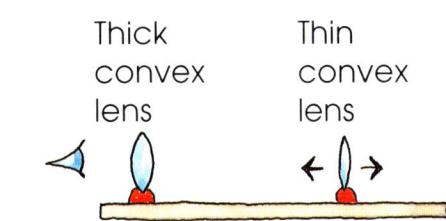

Thick convex lens

Thin convex lens

2. Fix the thick lens upright to one end of the piece of wood with plasticine.

3. Looking through the thick lens, slide the thin lens up and down the wood. When you can look through both lenses and see the wall on the other side of the room clearly, fix the thin one in position with plasticine.

4. Move your telecope further away from the wall. Does this make any difference to what you can see?

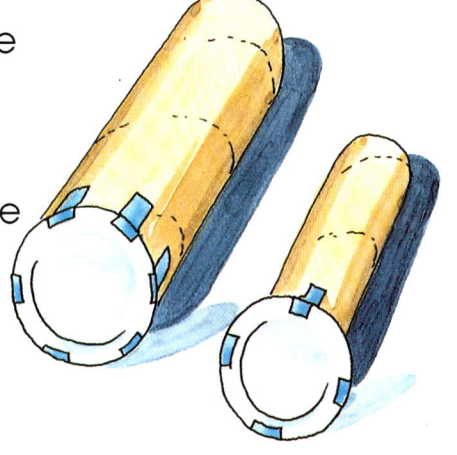

5. Now take the lenses off the piece of wood. Fix the thin lens to one end of the wider tube and the thick lens to one end of the narrower tube. Push the open end of this tube into the wider tube.

6. Look through the thick lens at the wall. Move one tube inside the other until you get a clear picture.

25

STARTING TECHNOLOGY

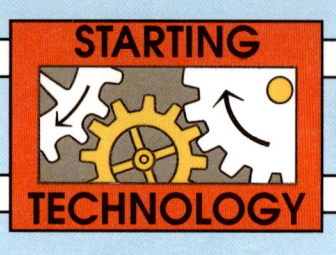

PLAYING WITH LIGHT

Making a flick book

You will need:

Thick paper
Scissors
Felt-tip pens
Glue
A stapler

1. Cut out several pieces of thick paper, about 12 cm long and 6 cm wide.

2. Draw a picture of a person running on each piece of paper. Each picture should show a different stage in the movement.

3. Fix the papers together to make a book with glue and a staple.

4. When you flick through the book, the person will seem to be moving.

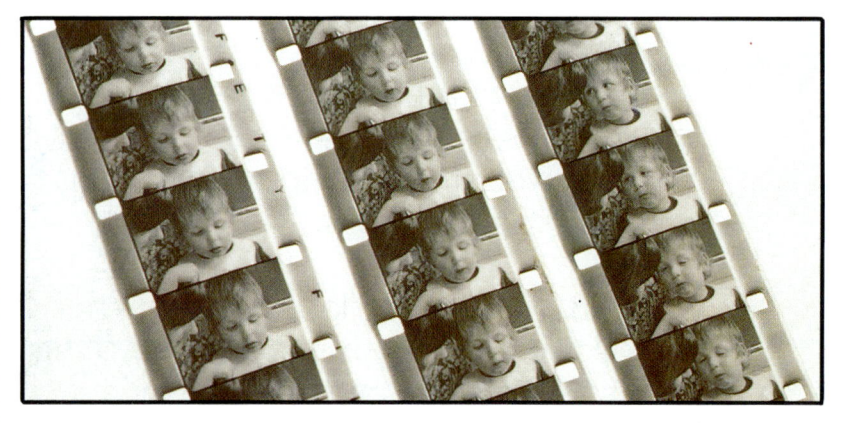

These are strips of film for showing at a cinema. They are put through a projector so quickly that the pictures seem to move.

A fish in a bowl

You will need:

Paper
Scissors
Felt-tip pens
A piece of dowel
Glue

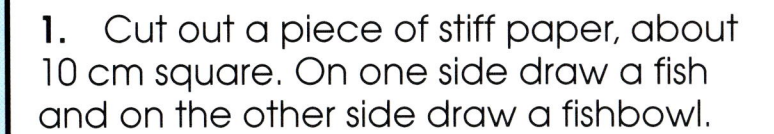

1. Cut out a piece of stiff paper, about 10 cm square. On one side draw a fish and on the other side draw a fishbowl.

2. Glue the paper to the end of the dowel.

3. Spin the dowel. As the paper spins the fish will seem to be in its bowl.

Mirror tricks

You will need:

Paper
Pens
A mirror

1. Write some large letters on a piece of paper.

2. Put the edge of the mirror beside them, so that it reflects the letters. Do some of the letters look different in the mirror? Do some look the same?

3. Put the edge of the mirror through the middle of the letters. Look at the patterns it makes.

27

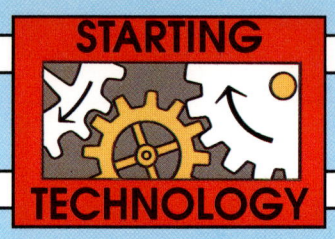

Notes for Parents and Teachers

SCIENCE

This book is concerned with designing and making models which use light and colour. Children can also, however, be allowed to experience situations which will begin to show them that colour and light are simply different aspects of the same phenomenon. Children at this age should not be expected to know about the behaviour of light in terms of waves or particles, but by playing and experimenting with mirrors they will begin to understand some of its properties.

DESIGN AND TECHNOLOGY

Children need to understand something of the nature of colour before they can begin to use it in the design process. The chapters in this book on tie-dye and shadow theatre are two projects where a greater understanding of the characteristics of light and colour will help. Children should be encouraged to use their scientific knowledge to identify and solve problems which arise.

LANGUAGE

Any science or technology topic will provide opportunities for children to extend their language skills. Seeing the image reflected in the bowl of a spoon is one such opportunity. Subjects such as this will give rise to much discussion which can lead to interesting creative and factual writing.

ART AND CRAFT WORK

It would be wrong to separate the science of colour from any painting or colouring that children do as part of their art work.

MATHEMATICS

Although there is less scientific testing involved in these models than in other books in this series, there is still a good deal of mathematics inherent in the work. Using mirrors, children will be involved in work on angles, shapes and symmetry. To make the models, children will need to measure accurately.

National Curriculum Attainment Targets

This book is relevant to the following Attainment Targets in the National Curriculum for **science**:

Attainment Target 1 (Exploration of science)   The designing, making and testing of all the models answer many of the requirements of this Attainment Target.

Attainment Target 15 (Using light and electromagnetic radiation)   All work on light and colour is relevant.

The following Attainment Targets are included to a lesser extent:

Attainment Target 2 (The variety of life)   Work on camouflage involves study of animals.

Attainment Target 6 (Types and uses of materials)   Work on tie-dye is especially relevant.

This book is relevant to the Attainment Targets in the National Curriculum for **technology**:

Attainment Target 1 (Identifying needs and opportunities)   Initial work on light and colours in this book involves children describing their surroundings and suggesting things to do. Projects such as making colour boxes and spinning circles involve using knowledge to discover opportunities for further work.

Attainment Target 2 (Generating a design)   Work on tie-dye involves proposing a design or pattern through drawings and using knowledge and skills to decide how to put it into practice. After making shadow theatres and projectors children will need to test and review their designs to see how to make them work better.

Attainment Target 3 (Planning and making)   All the projects in this book require children to choose and use suitable materials and tools.

Attainment Target 4 (Evaluating)   After making kaleidoscopes, periscopes, telescopes, projectors and shadow theatres children should judge how well their models have worked.

Teachers should also be aware of the Attainment Targets covered in other National Curriculum documents — particularly those for mathematics and language.

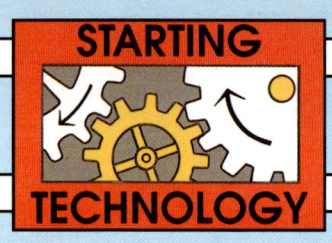

GLOSSARY

Camouflage The way animals hide themselves, usually by looking like other things near them.

Convex Curved outwards.

Diameter The length of a straight line going through the centre of a circle, from one side to the other.

Dowel A wooden rod.

Dyes Liquids used for colouring cloth or food.

Indigo A dark purply-blue colour.

Lenses Pieces of curved glass or plastic that can make beams of light bend.

Primary colours The main colours of light or painting. When mixed together they make other colours.

Prism A triangular-shaped see-through block. When you shine white light through it, the prism splits it into the seven colours of the rainbow.

Projector A machine that shines a light through a slide photograph and shows it as a big picture on a screen.

Rainbow An arch of different colours that you sometimes see in the sky. It happens when sunlight shines through raindrops.

Reflect To send back light from a shiny surface, such as a mirror, to give a picture.

Submarine A boat that can travel under water.

Transparent Completely see-through.

BOOKS TO READ

Animal Camouflage by Malcolm Penny (Wayland, 1987)
Colour by Terry Jennings (Oxford University Press, 1989)
Colours by Ed Catherall (Wayland, 1986)
Hide and Seek (Colour in Nature series) ed. by Jennifer Coldrey and Karen Goldie-Morrison (Andre Deutsch, 1986)
Let's Look At Colours by Constance Milburn (Wayland, 1988)
Light by Kay Davies and Wendy Oldfield (Wayland, 1991)
Light by Brenda Walpole (Kingfisher, 1987)
Light by Angela Webb (Franklin Watts, 1987)
Light and Dark by Ed Catherall (Wayland, 1985)
Mirrors and Lenses by Ed Catherall (Wayland, 1986)

Picture acknowledgements
The publishers would like to thank the following for allowing their photographs to be reproduced in this book: Chapel Studios 9, 11, 26; Eye Ubiquitous 16, 18, 22; Oxford Scientific Films 12; Science Photo Library 4; Tony Stone Worldwide 6; Timothy Woodcock 20. Cover photography by Zul Mukhida.

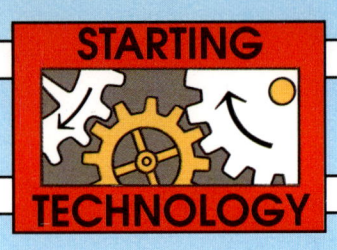

INDEX

camouflage 12-13
cinema 26
colour boxes 8

dyes 7, 14-15

films 26
flick books 26

glass 5, 9, 16

kaleidoscopes 16, 17

lenses 24, 25
   convex lenses 25

magnifying glasses 22, 23
microscopes 24
mirrors 16-19, 27
   curved mirrors 16

painting 6-7
patterns 5, 9, 11, 15, 16
periscopes 18-19
primary colours 5, 6, 7
prisms 5
projectors 22-3, 26

rainbows 4

shadows 5, 20-21
shadow theatres 21
slides 22-3
spectacles 9
spinning circles 10-11
spinning tops 11
submarines 18
sunlight 4, 6

telescopes 24, 25
tie-dye 14-15
transparency 5

windows 5, 9